QED START Maths

Measuring
Book 1

Ann Montague-Smith

QED Publishing

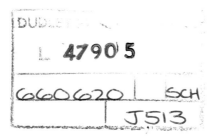

A Catalogue record for this book is available from the British Library.

ISBN 1-84538-027-4

Written by Ann Montague-Smith
Designed and edited by The Complete Works
Illustrated by Jenny Tulip
Photography by Steve Lumb and Michael Wicks

Creative Director Louise Morley
Editorial Manager Jean Coppendale

Printed and bound in China

With thanks to:

Contents

Big and little

Point to the big bears.

Now point to the little bears.

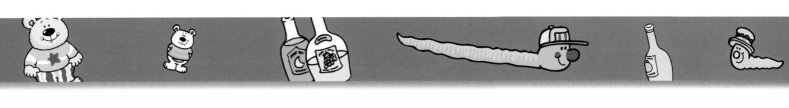

Challenge

Find some bears of different sizes. Which bears are big? Which bears are little? Now choose 2 of your bears. Which bear is bigger? Which bear is smaller?

5

Long, short, wide and narrow

Which are the long dogs?
Which are the short dogs?

long

wide

short

narrow

Which dogs are wide?
Which dogs are narrow?

Challenge

Find a long and wide dog. Now look for a dog which is long and narrow. Which dogs are short and wide?

High and low

What can you see high up?

What can you see low down?

8

Challenge

Look around the room you are in. Find 2 things that are high up. Now find 2 things that are low down.

Longer and shorter

Which worms are longer than Wiggly Worm?

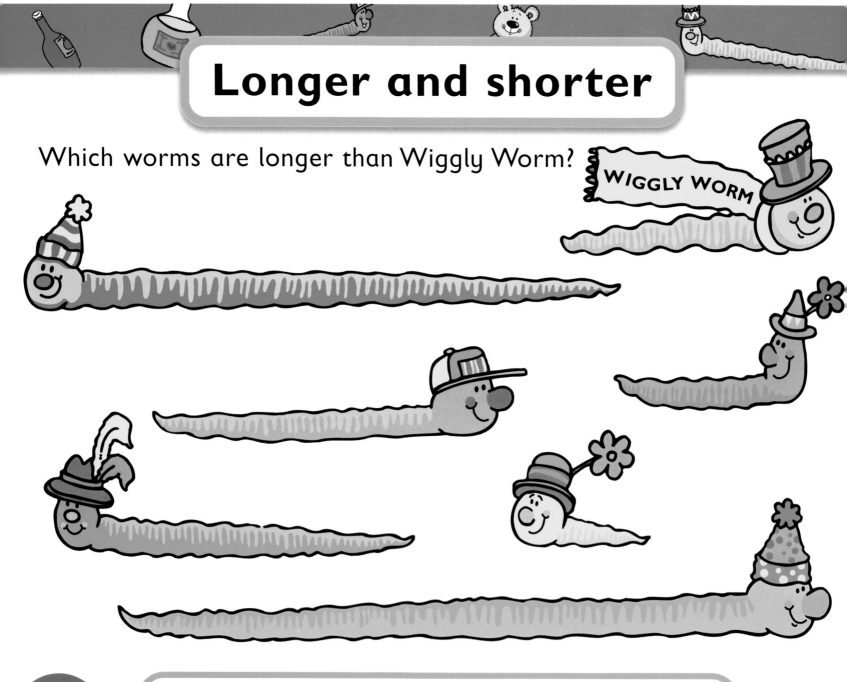

Which worms are shorter than Wiggly Worm?

Challenge

You will need some plasticine.
Make a worm. Make another
one that is longer. Now make
a worm that is shorter.
Can you put the worms in
order of length?
Start with the shortest worm.

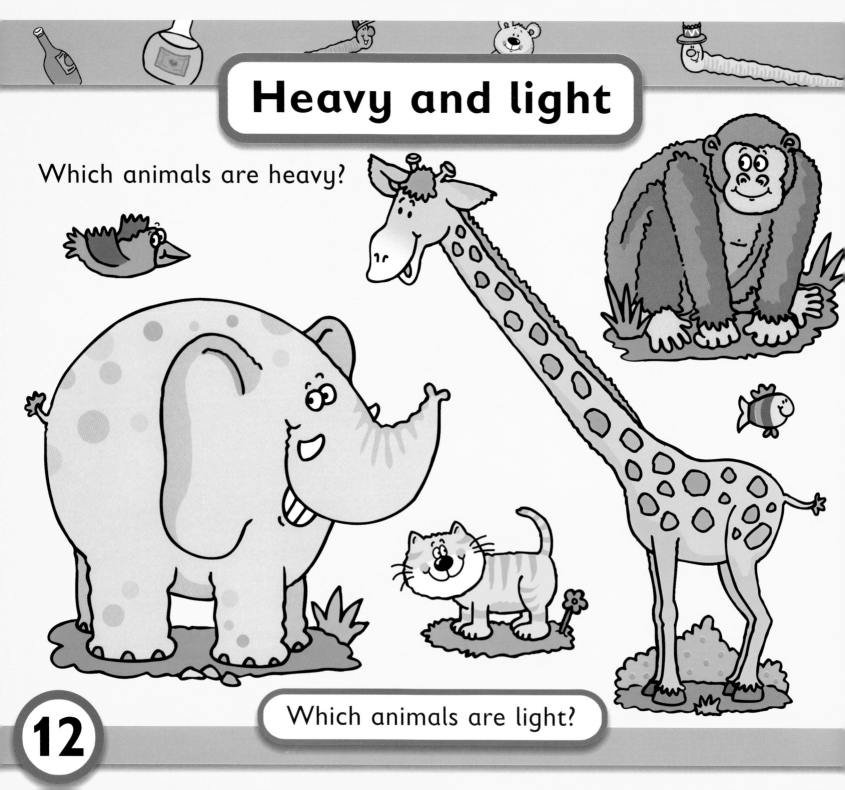

Heavy and light

Which animals are heavy?

Which animals are light?

Challenge

Choose some things in the room you are in. Sort out the heavy things. Sort out the light things.

Heavier and lighter

Point to the heavier toy.

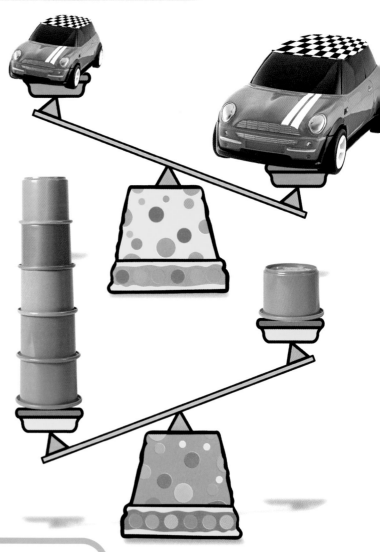

Which toy is lighter?

Challenge

Do this with a friend. Choose 2 toys. Decide which toy is heavier by holding them. Now check by putting the toys onto a balance.

Full and empty

Point to the bottles which are full.

Now point to the bottles which are not full.
Which ones are empty?

Challenge

You will need some dry sand.
Find some things to fill.
Fill them up.
Make them empty.
Now make them half full.

17

Which holds more?

Point to the one that holds more.

Now point to the one that holds less.

Challenge

You will need some dry sand and 2 different pots. By pouring sand, find out which pot holds more. So which pot holds less?

19

I know about the words...

You will need some counters.

Listen to the words.

Put a counter on the picture that matches.

holds more

holds less

little

big

wide

wider

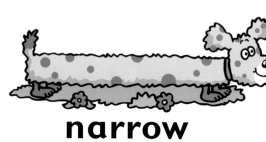

narrow

narrower

long

longer

short

shorter

full

empty

heavy

light

heavier

lighter

21

Supporting notes for adults

Big and little – pages 4-5

Talk about the bears on the page. Encourage the children to decide
which is 'big' and which is 'little'. Ask, 'Why do you think that?'

Long, short, wide and narrow – pages 6-7

The children may not agree on which is long/short/wide/narrow.
Encourage them to explain why they have made their choice.

High and low – pages 8-9

If the children are unsure of 'high' and 'low', encourage them to stretch up high, then
bend down low as you say these words. Then ask them to touch something high up in
the room, such as a point as high up the wall as they can reach, then low down, such as the floor.

Longer and shorter – pages 10-11

If children find making comparisons of length difficult, show them how to put a
piece of string along Wiggly Worm, then cut off the string to Wiggly's length.
Now they can use the string to compare the other worms' lengths.

Heavy and light – pages 12-13

If the children are unsure about the vocabulary, put out some items for the children to hold. Ask, 'Is this heavy?' 'Which one is light?'

Heavier and lighter – pages 14-15

If the children are unsure about which side of the balance shows 'heavier' and which 'lighter', use a balance with some toys. Talk about how the heavier side moves 'down' and the lighter side 'up'. Challenge the children to say what would happen if the 2 toys were about the same weight, then demonstrate this with 2 identical toys.

Full and empty – pages 16-17

If the children are unsure of the vocabulary, demonstrate full, empty and has some in – using sand or water and some containers.

Which holds more? – pages 18-19

If children do not understand about holding more and less, use some dry sand or water and some containers. Give the children time to pour from one container to the other. Ask, 'Did all the sand fit?' 'So which one holds more/less?'

I know about the words... – pages 20-21

Read the words under the pictures. Ask the children to say which picture shows that word. Encourage the children to show you which part of the picture depicts each idea.

Suggestions for using this book

Children will enjoy looking through the book and talking about the colourful pictures. Sit somewhere comfortable together. Please read the instructions to the children, then encourage them to take part in the activity and check whether or not they have understood what to do.

When comparing two things for length, ask 'Which is longer or shorter… wider or narrower?' for each pair. Check that the children do make a direct comparison. They will need to make sure that one end of both objects are level, so placing them on a table, or side by side, will help.

The images in the book can be used as starting points, so that the children go away to try some comparing of lengths, weights or capacities. Encourage them always to make a guess first, so that they are making an estimate. An estimate is never wrong, but it can always be improved in accuracy through checking by measuring.

If there is no bucket balance handy for the children to make comparisons of weight, they could use kitchen scales, but will then need some help in interpreting this. It is easier for the children to see what is happening if a two-pan set of kitchen scales can be used.

In capacity, where children are filling and pouring from containers, they may need reminding that in everyday life we do not fill things to the brim. Encourage them to talk about what would happen if we tried to drink from a cup full to the brim. However, when filling and pouring, and especially when using dry sand, children will want to fill to the brim.